First published 1987 by Walker Books Ltd
184-192 Drummond Street, London NW1 3HP

© 1987 Tony Wells

First printed 1987
Printed in Hong Kong by South China Printing Co.

British Library Cataloguing in Publication Data
Wells, Tony
Allsorts.
1. Picture puzzles – Juvenile literature
I. Title
793.73   GV1507.P47
ISBN 0-7445-0779-0
ISBN 0-7445-1013-9   Pbk

Allsorts

Tony Wells

WALKER BOOKS

LONDON

All these things are blue.

How many blue things in this picture?

7

All these things are soft.

Find the soft things on this beach.

Yum, yum! These are things to eat.

What could you eat at this picnic?

All these things are round.

How many round things in this picture?

All these things can fly.

How many of these things can fly?

All these things keep you warm.

Sort out the warm things in this scene.

All these things have stripes.

Sort out the striped things in this picture.

All these things are red.

How many red things in this picture?

All these things are spotted.

Find all the spotty things in this picture.

All these things have handles.

Find the things with handles in this garden.

All these things are square.

Sort out the square things for the magician.

All these things make a noise.

How many noisy things in this picture?